T0110738

Prophet
A View of the Suffering

ANGELIQUE MARTIN

WESTBOW
PRESS
A DIVISION OF THOMAS NELSON

WestBow Press books may be ordered through booksellers or by contacting:

WestBow Press
A Division of Thomas Nelson
1663 Liberty Drive
Bloomington, IN 47403
www.westbowpress.com
1-(866) 928-1240

Because of the dynamic nature of the Internet, any web addresses or links contained in this book may have changed since publication and may no longer be valid. The views expressed in this work are solely those of the author and do not necessarily reflect the views of the publisher, and the publisher hereby disclaims any responsibility for them.

Any people depicted in stock imagery provided by Thinkstock are models, and such images are being used for illustrative purposes only.

Certain stock imagery © Thinkstock.

ISBN: 978-1-4497-5770-0 (sc)
ISBN: 978-1-4497-5769-4 (e)

Library of Congress Control Number: 2012911558

Printed in the United States of America

WestBow Press rev. date: 08/08/2012

June 1, 2001

I dedicate this effort to my father,
Clifford L. Scott Sr.,
who steadily pushed me to complete
my education.
Thanks, Pops, for helping me obtain
my childhood dream.

To my God-given mentors,
Dr. Ann and Pastor Herman McCraw,
who encouraged me in and through
my "fears"
of accepting and standing as
God's Prophet.

CONTENTS

INTRODUCTION

This is a project to explore the topic of the Prophet as a present day, existing gift from Jesus and the believability of the office in the body of the Christian church. To begin the undertaking of this composition, a short general outlook of the Prophet will be presented.

My aim is to look into the Old Testament and New Testament structures, comparing any relationship or contrasting any difference. Lacking knowledge and understanding of the background of the Old Testament Prophet and the employment by God as a communicator of divine utterance very well may have hindered the New Testament Prophet from functioning in this present day. The Christian community today aligns the New Testament Prophet within the standards of the Old Testament Prophet thus giving value to disregard and to look down upon the Prophet. We will also look at the controls put upon the New Testament Prophet as it relates to what "type" of direction is to be performed. Present day measures tend to put the Prophet in a box or maintain limitations when scripture does not specifically state this was God's design. If we look at this mode of thought, it could be said the same is done to God and His desires for the Church and on an individual basis.

Exploration of each system of revealed commands will enlighten believers and the world that each range or scope of the Prophet can be unique in its origin and fulfillment. Then focusing upon the sensitive area of prophecy, I will inquire into the identity, nature and value of prophecy and the realm at which time prophecy is to be revealed. Many a Christian and or Christian community have experienced havoc, ruin and waste because of an incorrect prophecy or explanation, even though the acceptance and explaining of a prophecy is not the responsibility of the Prophet.

Along side the communication of the divine is timing. People may look at the area of timing, as it relates to giving a prophecy, but some avoid this vital necessity due to a lack of understanding or just being over zealous in the desire to speak forth for God. The operation of timing is also contained within the control and maturity of the Prophet. It is enough to say this subject is crucial to the well being of the body of Christ and God's creation as a whole.

In another segment, we will look at the Office of the Prophet opposite the Person as the Prophet. An office can contain a person with a questionable motive or it could be the person is faulty in their operation of the office. The Person as the Prophet could have been placed in the position through the directive of another with a hidden or personal motive or could have begun their position before God's timing. Timing is the key to every area of dealings and completion of life. Scripture declares, "as long as the earth remains, seedtime and harvest will continue" (Genesis 8:22). On the condition of this statement, we can place all of life under this microscope. There is no event creation will experience that will not require planting a seed, making a decision, waiting for God's timing (bringing the request from the spiritual to the natural) then experiencing the harvest (that which is desired is now seen).

The Office of the Prophet is a position created and set in the Church, by Jesus, to assist in the Church's direction and government. Other offices Jesus situated in the Church body for governing purposes are the Apostle, Evangelist, Pastor and Teacher. I once heard from Pastor Carlton Pearson a description of the governing head of the Church (to the best of my recollection) as follows:

Apostle – is the thumb of the hand
who goes out to find new locations
to establish God's strongholds and congregations then set in place a
Shepherd so they can go in search
of the next locale.
Prophet – is the index finger to point
in the direction of God and help with
the understanding of His commands
and decrees.
Evangelist – is the middle finger
calling out to the lost and calling
back those who have strayed away.

Pastor – the ring finger that marries
the congregation to hold them steady
in the growth of God in the local
Church body.

Teacher – the pinky finger to grasp
hold with the Pastor to expand on
the Word at a level all will receive
and perform.

Again, this is a possible depiction of the positions of the five-fold ministry. For more information on the governing aspect, one good book I would recommend is *the Shepherding Flock:The Church Beyond 2000 AD by John McHatton*. I believe it can be helpful.

Like the other offices or gifts given to the Church (Ephesians 4:11), the Office of the Prophet should be understood to be what it is, a position. But leadership positions have the ability to be arranged in importance, as positional requirements are needed, to assist in whatever undertakings the position(s) has been included and as persons may desire. The Office of the Prophet has a specific function, as it relates to the Church, which will not be exhausted in this writing but a glimpse shall be presented to spur interest in its necessity as deemed by Jesus. Then, prayerfully, an open mind (thinking) to the awareness of Jesus' forethought may be created. Lastly, the desire is to show that Jesus is the same from generation, to generation to generation (Hebrews 13:8). This office of and in the scheme of God has not diminished in practice since the first associated representation in the writing of scripture.

The opposing issue, in this comparison, is contained in the Person of the Prophet. A Prophet, as it relates to the person or the human being, have their own unique subject matter. Contained within the (human) being is the area of one's mindset, values, background(s), tradition(s) and, of course, the actual "flesh" body. It has been said through the years, the person (of the Prophet) receives a perfect message only to, possibly, relay it with flaws. Still others have felt to accept prophecy in its "raw" form could be receiving doubt and or inaccuracy.

This clouded view comes through many years of mistrust. People have used the Prophet for direction when individuals should have looked to

Jesus, first, with confirmation from the Prophet. This view also comes from misuse of the office, by the person called to be the Prophet, who may manipulate people in church authority, congregations, thus causing discord, and for dishonest gain.

The meaning of the title "office" is not, to a large extent, one and the same with this present age and the era in which the Bible was written. Language from where the Bible evolved to this present age may express its concept altogether opposite. The understanding from the past to the present could very well be the determining factor on the correct management of the aim of the office, and standards have tremendously changed since the beginning.

So in this chapter it is hoped each of us can think again about the Office of the Prophet versus the Person of the Prophet and be more knowledgeable about our relationship in and with Jesus alongside these two issues.

Chapter five will explore an assertion made by Jesus to His contemporaries – "A Prophet is not without honour, save in his own country, and in his own house"(Matthew 13:57) or "A Prophet is not without honour, but in his own country, and among his own kin, and in his own house"(Mark 6:4). Consideration of Christ's statement is worth mentioning today to involve and encourage the body of believers to more readily realize and value the necessity to accept God's choices of a person as a Prophet. While one's peers do not, at all times, recognize the importance of the status of the Prophet, God chooses whom He will give glory and honor. His positioning of persons, since He is more aware of what a person is capable of and what He has placed in the person, is done for the need of the body of believers and its ultimate unity. The title of this chapter, "Unwelcome" may clue one onto the area of focus. However, should this word and concept find itself contained within the body of believers? Scripture states, "For there is no respect of persons with God"(Romans 2:11) and believers will receive this revelation with open arms and hearts. Unfortunately, this revelation does not take in the leaders God has chosen in the believers' minds. "Respect of persons" does away with more people and blessings causing believers to question God why it occurs, without accepting responsibility for the rejection. However God is merciful and does not permit the unwanted to torment oneself for a long time, because of His love.

Rounding out the opinion, we will empower the public to voice their opinions, thoughts and conclusions. Many leaders of the Christian community and other religions have discussed their vast knowledge for world review; thus, it would be appropriate to include these persons who have the ability to understand additionally the true nature of the issue. Some of the contributors have first hand awareness in a variety of standpoints, thereby compelling the avenue of expression to be opened.

My desire is that your interest is stirred up and this book appeals to your thirst for wide-ranging information, not just to question as to the soundness of the presentation, but to produce added passion for investigation.

Books, essays, arguments or studies can provide an ignition to the vehicles of knowledge, understanding and wisdom. The greatest of these keys is God's Holy Word. So as the "keys to life" provide growth and exploration, may these pages produce the same corresponding treasures.

CHAPTER ONE

Prophet

The Christian community, in many cases, understands the Person as the Prophet and the Office of Prophet to be identical in operation, existence and experience in both the Old Testament and the New Testament. Then there are among the Christian body those that feel there are no revelations or discoveries happening in this present day. Such disbelief and doubt may be due to errors committed by false Prophets of today, so therefore when a "true" Prophet of God speaks he or she also is rejected. To compound the issues, along with the true Prophet being rejected, the truth is rejected.

People reject truth for various reasons. The main reason is because the truth could cause pain and what society runs from and resists most, change. In society today it may be, to some, easier to accept present conditions or error than to take a stance on an issue. But the Prophet is called to stir up issues, is requiring persons to take a stand against error, which could cause more rejection by the church community. Could we therefore say that Prophets are God's "shakers and movers?" God has called Prophets to provoke a shaking up of the self-satisfied, moving the dead in spirit and causing motivation. I'd say they are causing a reaction like the day that the earth rocked on that historic day at Calvary.

This is the call and choice of the Prophet. The call since the Prophet was chosen by God is to assist in recognizing errors in His children, give guidance to His children in the thoughts and ways of Himself and to assist in working out correction. Man is a free-will agent and he has the choice, the ability and right to choose to accept or reject the "calling" of the Almighty.

Just the same, the Church community has the ability and right to accept or reject the likelihood of the Prophet in the modern Church.

The acceptance or rejection of the Prophet can also be based in part upon the remaining five-fold ministries.[1] The Apostle, Evangelist, Pastor and Teacher, attaching importance to the Prophet, open the door for the Prophet to operate freely, but their negative reaction hinders the free flow of the gift, the Prophet.

Ephesians chapter four and verse twelve provides the intention for each office and elder of the church, as it relates to the growth and unity within the church. Jesus' well-constructed, structure for the directing of believers, providing needed knowledge, growth, unity, and the continued bringing together of God's creation to Himself was created and given by Jesus. Having endless understanding and insight to the corruption of unconditional power in the control of perverted and unskilled man, this check and balance, through the counsel of elders, was constructed.

Contained within this check and balance structure is the Prophet. The Prophet, like the others (gifts from Jesus), carries unique duties and giftings and is given distinct qualifications and assignments. The Prophet is situated to assist in the administration of the church alongside the other four offices of the five-fold ministries; and again they are instituted to encourage accountability and to add checks and balances.

The office contains a person understood to have the "ear" of God; consultations or spiritual guidance are advised to assist in directions and directives, as given in the example of the Old Testament judges and counsels. Jethro gave good, godly counsel to Moses[2] to assist him in the daily service and support of the nation of Israel. So Jesus' intent is to continue this structure of church leadership within the New Testament Church, through the Prophet, to obtain good, godly counsel. Thus we are going to explore the Prophet in the framework of the Old Testament and New Testament, looking for similarities and perhaps contrasts. Investigating the person called to be a Prophet, our intent is to see what motivates them to accomplish the calling of God. Can we uncover the need to speak forth and

---

[1] Ephesians 4:11
[2] Exodus 18:19-23

declare what they "hear" or become aware of within? Can we understand what propels them to share and declare what wells up within their spirit; that which is understood to be the announcements of God?

The Prophet's divinely ordained position carries the added call assignment to reconcile the church to each other, as well as the Church to God. Alongside the genuine Prophet, the Prophet's instruction, direction and rebuke have opened an endless level of debate with the entrance of false Prophets and those looking to "fleece the flock", for a price and fame.

As a result why do the church and/or people reject Prophets and the existence of the office in the present day church as a likely and workable office and as an official officer and elder? Is there no evidence of the true and genuine Prophet to compel the Church to believe Jesus' creation of the office and called those of His children? Has the Office passed away? What are some of the misunderstandings of the Prophet and the Office? Is prophecy truly to be feared?

In a brief examination of the Old Testament and New Testament Prophet, their functions and Prophecy, it is a desire that we may see where the church has strayed or been led to reject the Prophet. In each book of the Synoptic Gospels (Matthew, Mark and Luke) the rejection issue was revived to present that, as it has been said for generations, from the Old Testament, to Jesus and today, "there is nothing new under the sun." From the time of Moses, the children of Israel have rejected the Prophet. But this has not been the desire of the Almighty God. He came to the people He chose, raised up amongst them what and whom they needed and demanded, but just as Israel and the Modern Church reject God and knowledge[3], so they reject the Prophet.

In light of these issues and declarations, my desire is these statements will open our minds to "hear" the thoughts and intents presented.

Ultimately the church, hopefully, is looking to come into the unity of the faith. But this accomplishment will not appear until there is no longer a need for the "gifts" from Jesus, which includes the Prophet.

---

[3] Hosea 4:6

CHAPTER TWO

Old Testament Prophet
versus
New Testament Prophet

In its original terms, design and understanding, Prophet had a non-gender bias (or leaning) and thus the office and title made reference to both male and female, with no prejudice. The term was applied to individuals who gave significant military and judicial (officially authorized) leadership. Each one also had heavenly or spiritual contact with God and expressed this experience through worship and songs of victory[4]. Moses and Deborah are examples. Moses was called by God to obtain the release of God's chosen nation from the bondage of Egypt, while Deborah led Barak and the army of ten thousand (10,000) men from the tribes of Naphtali and Zebulum upon Mount Tabor and defeated the Canaanites who were oppressing Israel. The groups and names given to identify Prophets had a wide variety from generation to generation. With these groups and names came ranges of status and Moses has been singled out as the standard for the Prophet of the spokesman category.

Nabi (naw-bee'), from the root word NABA (naw-bah), means, "*to bubble forth as a fountain.*" This definition brings to mind the thought that the words received by and through the Prophet were unexpected. Thus the content appears to have been unknown prior to the moment. The name

---

[4] The Eerdmans Bible Dictionary, Allen C. Myers, ed. p. 852.

Nabi was in circulation as far back as the Pentateuch (the first five books of the Bible) and existed before, after and alongside the two other Hebrew words for Prophet, ROEH (ro'eh) and CHOZEH (kho-zeh'). The Nabi Prophet was the spokesmen for God and was the go-between for God <u>to</u> man. This type of Prophet was also someone who spoke for another human, such as Aaron for Moses.

The next Hebrew labeling and name is ROEH, *a seer*, from the word RA'AH (raw-aw') that means *to see*. This term was widespread in Samuel's day[5]. This word appears ten times in scripture; seven of the references are to Samuel.[6]

Our last word is CHOZEH, which also means *seer*, and it became common when Roeh was becoming less used and the return of Nabi began. Chozeh comes from the more charming word CHAZEH (khaw-zeh). Chazeh, also, means *to see*, and the person was considered one who kept an eye upon the spiritual world. So it was associated with Prophets in a "prophetical (visionary or far-sighted) revelation" category in the Pentateuch and the books of Samuel, Chronicles and Job.

An early account or meaning of the word "Prophet" was *"one protected by God in a special way."* Later, during the Monarchic period (the period of Emperors and Kings), more accepted descriptions were a seer or one who hears from God, but the pre-monarch versions were still given and understood, as stated in the Hebrew references above. During the monarch era's entrance came the more commonly accepted definition of Prophet, a "Seer". Elijah, Elisha and Nathan were in this category. Also during this age of Kings, came the development of Old Testament religion and the "canonical (law or rule) book of the Prophet." The list of these types of Prophets contains the likes of Gad, who advised King David; Isaiah, who ministered under four kings, and Jeremiah, who ministered during the reign of five kings.

Prophets were called to advise in matters of the state, and, as such, some kings only responded or reacted after the Prophet's words of advice. In some cases hatred and ill feelings existed, between the Prophets and the kings,

---

[5] I Samuel 9:9
[6] Fausset, A. R., Bible Cyclopaedia

because of the refusal to accept the Prophets by the Kings, but Prophets remained and were respected based on their need and usefulness; i.e. their ability to hear from God.

With the refusal to accept the Prophets came the "portrayal" (illustration or acting out) of prophecy, by select individual Prophets, and because of that the Prophet was identified with his or her message. God used these select Prophets to make known the "false" Prophets sending out words of peace. The "true" Prophet's description of future exile and being in prison, coupled with forms of control, stood as a public announcement of God's wrath against the people's disobedience. The Prophet was God's mouthpiece when man's ears were on purpose closed.

In God's permitting Kings to stand as ruler over His children, God maintained His greatest and highest position as King of the government and His dominion. Because of the weakness and shortcoming of man and his leaning to sin and greed, when Kings were selected, through the Prophets, God put out of use, expressed disapproval, encouraged, set up or put down kings. In times when Kings had left behind or had forgotten the children of God and the King had forgotten his previous loyalty, God made stronger, in the faith, the scattered remnant of believers.

God still uses His Prophets in the church today in the same manner as mentioned before during the times of Emperors and Kings. This is not the normal role of Prophets but the exception. The function of the Prophet in directing an individual, groups or leaders is not always public, but privately as it relates to disobedience, to provide the hearer the possibility to repent. But when a person or leader refuses to listen to a Prophet to turn from what is against God's will, God may, in a public fashion, bring to light a transgression; again this would be for the express purpose of repentance, as did Nathan to David.

Prophets proclaimed much to the people as God directed them, and it included many future events, thus seer. Just a note of interest, and a little known fact, is that the command or decree of the addition of the Gentiles was first preached by Old Testament Prophets even though it looks like it is focused upon in the New Testament.

Prophetes (prof-ay'-tace) is the Greek replacement for the Hebrew Nabi. It's root lies in *pro* and *phemi7* (fay-mee') which means, *"speak forth"* *truths for another*, so it can be defined *interpreter*. In some circles prophetes is understood as "passive" (agreeable, yielding, submissive or consenting), with the connection being one chosen by God specifically for the task, but more commonly thought to be "active" (practicing or involved), one who declares or preaches.

New Testament Prophets are modeled after Old Testament Prophets in that the Spirit of God inspires them, and divine inspirations occur through the same channel[8], love.

Jesus is described several times as a Prophet in the Scriptures, though the term is used with various differences. Mark's writings have Jesus being a Prophet along the line of an eschatological[9] prophetic figure[10] while in Matthew twenty-one, the people proclaimed him a Prophet as He entered Jerusalem, which caused fear in the Pharisees because of the crowd.

But is seems the doctor, Luke, had the most in-depth understanding and grasp of the eschatological Prophet, Jesus. In Luke chapter seven, verse sixteen, Jesus is understood to be working as a Prophet due to His raising of the young man of Nain. Chapter seven and verse thirty-nine makes obvious Jesus' miraculous foreknowledge as a prophetic gift. Finally, chapter twenty-four, verse nineteen, sums up Jesus' entire presence and character as that of a Prophet mighty in word and deed before God and the people. Luke, the author of book of Acts, had an insight as it relates to the coming out of Prophets as being a sign of the eschatological outpouring of the Spirit. Basically he felt all Christians have the gift of prophecy[11], but Paul in First Corinthians contradicts this belief with the statement:

---

[7]   Andrew Robert Fausset, Bible Cyclopaedia, p. 584
[8]   I Corinthians 13:2
[9]   The branch of theology that is concerned with the end of the world or of humankind. A belief or a doctrine concerning the ultimate or final things, such as death, the destiny of humanity, the Second Coming, or the Last Judgment
[10]   Exegetical Dictionary of the New Testament, Horst Balz and Gerhard Schneider, Editors, 183-186
[11]   Exegetical Dictionary of the New Testament, 183-186

> So God has appointed some in the
> church [for His own use]: first apostles (special messengers); second
> prophets (inspired preachers and expounders)
> third teachers; then wonder-workers;
> then those with ability to heal the sick; helpers; administrators;
> [speakers in] different (unknown) tongues. Are all apostles (special
> messengers)? Are all prophets (inspired interpreters of the
> will and purposes of God)? Are all
> teachers? Do all have the power of performing miracles? Do all possess
> extraordinary powers of healing?
> Do all speak with tongues? Do all interpret?[12]

Another impression of the modern church is the understanding of what the Prophet is to communicate in their prophecy. Prophecies heard take on many characteristics, both then and now. According to Paul in First Corinthians fourteen, verses three and thirty-one, New Testament Prophets are called to edification (up-building), exhortation (constructive spiritual progress), comfort (encouragement and consolation) and persuasion (have an affect on) of unbelievers. But before continuing, the one-dimensional meaning of edification, exhortation, comfort and persuasion is what the church believes the Prophet only is to proclaim which causes many areas of debate. It is not to our benefit or the Prophet's freedom to function in the church body to let stand the above "narrow" definitions. The Prophet's full ability to function is reduced and weakened, without exploration of these words, their function has not come to be understood and neither is possible unless deeper study is done.

The following definitions were taken from Merriam Webster's Collegiate[13] dictionary to aide in a deeper insight and study of what God has asked His Prophet to do while contained within the same outer wear (skin) that the persons receiving live.

Edification has its root in edify. This message is more along the line of classroom instruction. It means to instruct or improve spiritually, build, establish, uplift, enlighten and inform. The Prophet is using the Word to

---

[12] I Corinthians 12:28-30, Amplified

[13] Merriam Webster's Collegiate Dictionary, tenth edition, Merriam-Webster's Collegiate Inc., copyright 1997, principal copyright 1993.

bring about the rebuilding of a life, as with the change of heart of unbelievers, and then instructing the church to develop beyond milk (being child-like or young) and go from awareness to awareness.

Exhortation in its root term is to exhort. The definition is to give rise to a decision or inflame by argument or advice, to urge strongly, to give warnings and make urgent appeals. Thus the second expression has an instruction requiring an immediate response by the hearer and the directive may be given as correction for disobedience or being slothful.

The definition of comfort is twofold and is clearer if we take them one at a time. First, comfort is to give strength and hope, to ease grief or trouble, with an identical meaning of soothe or raise someone's spirit, which means ease the grief or sense of loss or trouble. This brings to mind the added duty of counseling. Then encourage is the second part of comfort. Its definition is to inspire with courage, spirit or hope, to spur on, stimulate and to give help or support to one; a scope of meaning often misunderstood by many believers.

Lastly, there is persuade and persuasion. First persuade is to successfully urge somebody to perform a particular action, especially by reasoning, pleading, or coaxing and to assist in accepting something given the Prophet by God, especially by giving good reasons for accepting the command or directive. Finally, persuasion is the ability to persuade persons in the direction requested by Father God. These understood or not so understood elements, features or callings are not the sum total of the New Testament Prophet's call, but are taught in some circles as the criteria to "measure" the evidence of the office.

To be a Prophet one must first be called to the Office of the Prophet, which is to be a Minister of the Gospel and separate oneself unto God. He or She is not a "layman" or one not skilled in the Word of God. They are developed in the word and also must meet the qualifications of an Elder. There are several levels, classifications and descriptions of Prophets, for the governing body, and the conditions to function in the capacity of the office (Prophet) in the church. But the need for spiritual maturity to fulfill the calling he or she is called upon to carry out cannot be stressed enough.

Many a person has gone the way of greed and pride to their own disadvantage and damage and the harm of family and community because of the misuse of the call, the lack of knowledge and preparation and spiritual immaturity.

The Scripture states the Holy Spirit distributes spiritual gifts or special abilities to each individual as He wills and in some cases will manifest multiple gifts through a person and calling. Some religious scholars believe a Prophet should have a constant display of at least two of the revelation gifts, word of wisdom, word of knowledge or discerning of spirits[14], along with prophecy[15]. This is not stated in scripture; however in theory it has soundness.

There is, however, a major difference in the calling of New Testament Prophets. Their focus is to preach and teach the Word of God. Prophecy, through the Prophet, is not the primary form of communication between God and His children since believers have the presence of Jesus through the indwelling (residing) of the Holy Spirit. In times past, in the Old Testament, the only communication with God was through the Prophet, but after the sacrifice of Jesus and the witness in the earth of the Holy Spirit, each believer has the right and ability to go directly to the throne of grace for themselves. God, in His infinite wisdom, has provided a source to confirm what a believer hears in his or her spirit, reads in the Word and receives during his or her prayer time. Thus the Prophet proclaims the Word of God to people in response to a divine call, with an urgency to speak for God, addressing the circumstance of the day and confirming what individuals have received. God's intent, with the dawning of the Prophet is to bring His people into agreement and fulfillment with the covenant and His will.

Prophets are God's divine instruments working in the church to create growth, to save the lost, to establish the kingdom (rule and reign) of God in the world, and proclaim the truths of God He is restoring that have been neglected. There are, in the book of Acts, Prophets specifically named that illustrated the works of the Holy Spirit and some of them were leaders in the local congregations. These Prophets and the Office are not said to have

---

[14] I Corinthians 12:8 and 10

[15] Kenneth E. Hagin, The Ministry Gifts, Fourth Edition, Oklahoma, Faith Library Publications, p. 28.

ceased in any capacity, but only mentioned, in significance, when needed or necessary.

The Office of the Prophet has no more significance than the other four gifts of Jesus.[16] The intent in this writing is to inform that the Office of the Prophet is still a realistic unit of the Church of Jesus Christ.

---

[16] Ephesians 4:11

CHAPTER THREE

Prophecy

Prophecy is the divinely prompted statement, expression or declaration of a Prophet given to a person, persons or congregation for the express purpose of communication from God. "The Spirit literally outfits Himself with the person and uses his of her "abilities" as instruments."[17]

The Greek word for prophecy is propheteia (*prof-ay-ti'-ah*). It is a gift changing one into God's mouthpiece and expressing His words as the Spirit directs. This gift is moreover the speaking forth of the mind and counsel of God.

The Book of Revelation states prophecy is "the testimony of Jesus is the spirit of prophecy."[18] So when one prophesies they are witnessing and giving evidence of Jesus. It is designed to unfold the beauty and loveliness of our Lord and, again, that Jesus is the common essence and theme of all prophecy. This address, too, is given out from divine inspiration to declare the purposes of God. Prophecies sometimes contain disapproval and warnings to the wicked, then comfort for the hurt and oppressed, while revealing the hidden foretelling of future events.[19]

Journeying forward, our focus will be on the act or action (performance) of prophecy. The action of prophecy in the Greek is propheteuo (*prof-ate-yoo'-o*). Here we more readily see the foretelling of events combined with

---

[17] Dr. Ann McCraw, lecture and lecture notes, Gifts of the Holy Spirit, Spring, 1998.

[18] Revelation 19:10

[19] Joseph H. Thayer, Thayer's Greek-English Lexicon of the New Testament

divine revelation, the drive to foretell: the breaking forth under sudden force in a grand message or in praise: the revealing of the unknown connected with other Holy Spirit gifts, such as the Word of Wisdom and the Word of Knowledge. God is subject to use prophecy with one or more of these additional gifts as an "attention" vehicle for the nonbeliever or the method of relationship to the believer, so one understands their importance to the Almighty God. However the Holy Spirit manifests Himself, the intent and understanding is to express that a divine, supernatural utterance has come from the mind of God.

With all this verbal expression, the question can be raised whether prophecy is different from preaching. To the one not in possession of the facts it could leave one in a difficult position. But to remove the clouds of doubt, each is separate of the other. Prophecy is not preaching and neither is preaching prophecy.

The individuality of prophecy is more explicit in the Greek language, without the hint of interchanging the words for prophecy or preaching. This difference, showing the Greek, is presented in the four ways prophecy is listed in First Corinthians chapter fourteen and verse six:

> Now brethren, if I come unto you
> speaking with tongues, what shall
> I profit you, except I shall
> speak to you either by revelation
> (apokalupsis [ap-ok-al'-oop-sis]),
> or by knowledge (ginosko [ghin-oce'-ko]),
> or by prophesying
> (propheteia [prof-ay-ti'-ah])
> or by doctrine (didache [did-akh-ay'])?
> and the two words used for
> preaching, euangelizo (yoo-an-ghel-id'-zo)
> (*proclaim the good news*)
> and kerusso (kay-roos'-so) (*herald*).[20]

---

20 Dr. Ann McCraw, lecture and lecture notes, Gifts of the Holy Spirit, Spring, 1998.

13

On the other hand, preaching can contain prophecy, but is not prophecy. Prophecy should never become a substitute for preaching and teaching.

Thus prophecy is uncommon to man's acquired abilities; a person can learn to preach and teach. Knowledge, too, can be obtained revelation knowledge and contain revelation hidden in one's study, the mysteries of the gospel. But the Holy Spirit, again, divinely inspires prophecy, with the vessel having no prior awareness of the content, except for the moment it is received.

It has been said over and over, that prophecy is a divine, supernatural declaration, but is it the truth or what is true prophecy? Can there be or is there an instrument to know when true prophecy is given? Yes. True prophecy exists when the declaration or statement exalts the divine being and sacrifice of Jesus the Christ. It will magnify Him in an assortment of avenues with the central theme being directed toward Jesus: the shedding of His blood and the encouragement to worship and praise His name; The proclamation of His ways, will and word; His compassion; Pleadings; and Tenderness. Prophecy always comes to the center of existence, Jesus.

This is why believers are given a warning to "despise not prophesyings."[21] Believers are not to make a mockery or treat with contempt the utterings (expressions, pronouncements, statements) of the Holy Spirit. To ignore or belittle prophecy is to hold back or restrain the Spirit. Another way it could be said, one has determined not to hear the chosen "mouth" of God from the midst of the assembly.[22] A failure to receive prophecy is to knowingly, and on purpose, refuse to hear God, Himself.

With the caution of Paul, in First Thessalonians, put forward it brings to question, "is prophecy valid for today?" Emphatically, yes! There are approximately thirty references to prophecy and prophesying as a continuing portion of the body. In the books of Joel and Acts there are references to prophecy in and to the present day.[23] And in First Corinthians chapter twelve the gifts of the Spirit are shown as given to the spiritual body of which one is prophecy.

---

[21] I Thessalonians 5:20
[22] Deuteronomy 18:15-22
[23] Joel 2:28 and Acts 2:16-18

Prophecy contains three major elements necessary to the Church body, edification, exhortation and comfort or cheer. In chapter two we stated the Prophet is called to provide these endowments, thus the essence of their message. Prophecy is spoken to build up believers, stir up believers and cheer them up to continue the purposes of God.

Lastly, after looking in the content and workings of prophecy, the timing of the deliverance of the prophecy cries to be mentioned. When is a prophecy to be spoken and what is its scope or range? Not all proclamations are for everyone and some statements are not to be given at that particular time frame. Many have come to error, hurt or ruin based on an incorrectly delivered or timed prophecy. The prophecy may not have been delivered promptly. The prophecy should not have been expressed verbally or should not have been delivered in a public arena.

When a prophet "hears" from the throne of God, it's believed they go through a "process of elimination." This process being internal with the expectation the timing issue would be included. But previously the statement was given the Prophet would not know when the prophecy would "appear" and that belief still stands. The Prophet at this point is questioning the process of elimination. The process of elimination being, to whom are the words directed, when is the prophecy to be given and how much of the prophecy is to be revealed? This, too, begs the question, "I thought they didn't know what was being said until that moment. Yes, again, that is true, but some prophecies are given just to the Prophet versus the sudden speaking forth type, "the bubbling forth." In the speaking forth of God's divine inspirations, the prophecy should fall into place, catch sight of and wait for the unction from the Holy Spirit. It is not required that prophecy goes forth at every gathering. Then, too, the person chosen may rotate from situation to situation, need to need and each vessel should maintain themselves as scripture dictates, "the spirits of the prophets are subject to the prophet."[24] Being cautious and prudent is admirable. God is not in a rush, so neither is there a necessity of the prophecy. Whatever God has to say to His children or child He can bring it out later if need be; then too,

---

[24] I Corinthians 14:32

the place or persons whereto the prophecy is meant may be unprepared or unwilling to receive.

When a person is given a prophecy it is for a time, season or event. Prophecy is not, usually, a "microwave" directive from God or given to be completed immediately. It is given to get a person, persons or church body to understand what God is and/or will do in and through them. The miracle realm is not part of prophecy's makeup. Prophecy, as stated earlier, is to proclaim the future. It is given to get one to believe and/or its completion is dependent on the receiver. It will come and take place because you are ready to go to the next level, to show you are on the correct path ordained by God, are in obedience, you will be going in a certain direction or to get you to accept the direction of God.

A word perceived in one's spirit, "the inner man" or the "voice" within, should be investigated as to the appropriate time to speak forth what is received. Timing is defined as when one is to say what one has heard, to whom is it directed and should the entire message be revealed.

God reveals what is needed at a given season to accomplish one's purpose, duties and one's destiny. But there are times some will not listen or be receptive to what God has to say or comprehend what God has said within the context of prophecy. Thus to assist in the lack of comprehension, the Prophet is given the anointing to present and/or confirm God's words, His heart and mind. Prophecy should not modify one's normal mode of communication with God, but utilized, in divine inspiration, as a tool of assistance in times of confusion and/or indecision.

Contained in the supremacy of God, is the possibility of the "absence of greater clarity" in prophecy from prophets. This is due to God's purpose to give light enough to guide the willing and to leave darkness enough to confound the willfully blind.[25]

Prophecy has a moral purpose and
mercifully gives God's loving, fatherly warning to
the non-repenting, that by turning from the violating
of His laws and obeying His commands and
directives they may turn aside righteous judgment.

---

[25] Andrew Robert Fausset, Bible Cyclopaedia, p. 585.

CHAPTER FOUR

Office of the Prophet
Opposite
The Person as the Prophet

The church may well accept the Office of the Prophet although the Church body can be neutral or unexcited in their acceptance. The office can be understood as an element or section of the Church, not contributing any significant contribution, and as such will cause no noticeable disturbance within the framework of a body of believers or congregation. Persons are likely to accept most any office or entity in a nonspecific expression. It is when the human factor, a person, is introduced to stand in an office that disagreement, debate and confusion materialize.

Following the rejecting of the Office of the Prophet, because of misunderstanding or disbelief, some will reject the office for the simple reason a particular individual has proclaimed to be called to the position. This state of mind that rejects prophets seems to be universal, among the spiritually discerning, and can be more widespread in secular society. It could be said, a lot of the world's thinking has "crept into the mind" of believers.

The understood meaning of Ephesians chapter four, verse twelve focuses on the office of the ministry or support. But the key to the word *office* in Paul's writings is "the work". An office in the Christian community, regardless of "status" (position or standing), includes the providing of service. This is the central theme of each of the offices given by Jesus to the body of Christ, but the evangelist's focus primarily can be on the lost creation of God. Paul also encouraged Timothy to do the works of an Evangelist in his calling as a Pastor, for the reason of serving the Christian community and those outside the body. This thought, alongside growth in the body, is the central subject matter of the Office of the Prophet, as well to work in the harvest.[26] Unfortunately, believers (the Church community) understand and are taught the office has passed away, but that thought, according to scripture, is not reality.

The Office of the Prophet is an official position and responsibility to the body of the Christ. When Jesus made available gifts to the Church body, His intent was and is the training of believers to agreement in thought and deed and their ultimate reward, but until the appearance of that day, the reward, the maturing of believers is of the utmost importance.

People associate the Office of the Prophet as a position or station in life to attain for identification. But each office of the five-fold ministries should be looked upon as equal in stature and as ministers containing the openness to receive the divine inspiration from God, for then this willingness will convert to ministering to believers and non-believers. The Office of the Prophet is, like all offices and believers, called to minister or care for the body of the Christ.

Diakonia[27] (dee-ak-on-ee'-ah) involves compassionate love towards those in need. Granted most perceive this compassionate love as serving and it is rendered in physical service. The scriptures state that one meaning of this Greek word denotes the concept of "waiting on tables" as in the Office of Deacon, but another concept states it is for the benefit of the proclamation of the gospel. This Greek word, diakonia, contains the essence of the official calling of leadership of the Office of the Prophet.

On the other hand, there are those who accept a person declaring to be called as a Prophet, but not the likelihood of the Office of the Prophet as a working entity in the body as a portion of the leadership.

The Person as the Prophet is one who "fights", verbally, for the oppressed, down trodden Christian and creation of God, in addition to God and

---

[26] Matthew 9:37

[27] Greek, meaning ministry, ministration; i.e. the office of ministering in divine things

His words and desire(s) to be heard and obeyed. God is ever presenting to His prophets the terrible and horrifying issues He hates. These same persons, when engaged in intercessory prayer, hear the cries of them calling upon the Almighty for rescue and relief. Contained within these chosen people, God's prophets, are fierce feelings and emotions, appropriate to the burden(s) thrust upon their soul and spirit by God; fitting to God's deep, severe love for his children.

A Person as the Prophet can be considered distant, detached and unfriendly in their behavior and conduct. This can be attributed to many hours of separation, seclusion and spending an immense amount of hours before God's face. Therefore the bulk of a Prophet's life of communion with God will be spent in prayer to hear the direction for God's children, standing in the stead for saved and unsaved individuals and for their own renewal. The Person as the Prophet, like the other gifts from Jesus, requires a larger portion of refreshing, because of the amount of persecution from the attacks of the enemy and demands from the body requiring or requesting assistance and attention.

The Office of the Prophet and the Person as the Prophet's existence are to serve and glorify God while imparting to believers. Due to this detached character, the Prophet's circle of relationships can be small, if not minute. Prophets do not choose to be withdrawn, but for the sake of the call and the needs of the body, they strive to be before the face of God immersed in His glory.

Lastly I want to stress, the Office of the Prophet and the Person as the Prophet have no more significance than any of the other positions in the leadership of the Church. This office and accepted calling, Office of the Prophet and the Person as the Prophet, are for the working of ministry in the proclaiming of the good news (gospel).

CHAPTER FIVE

Unwelcome

The acceptance of the Prophet can be likened to the relationship of children to parents and children to their peers.

Parents out of love and affection create and raise their children to continue the cycle of life, due to the inborn spirit to re-create themselves to continue the legacy. These parents are continually pouring into this new creation, knowledge, love, caring, instruction, money and any other life essentials for their children to continue and reproduce in like manner.

Joined in this ritual of existence was life growing among the town's people and neighbors. The environment being so knit together everyone knew everyone within the community. Some have had such friendships and relationships that they had spent days, maybe weeks, at a time at each other's home in fellowship. The children would have even had times of staying the night at a friend's home and sharing breakfast the next morning. Sharing the joys of childhood and getting to see the new mischief each would partake and hopefully skate the end result of corporal punishment if found out. There are members of this close-knit neighborhood, of the younger generation, slowing growing into teen years and amongst them some have become more infamous and dishonorable.

Through childhood and teenage years this child is known among the neighborhood and relatives as a troubled youth or the one that caused much grief and embarrassment for the family.

Parents, relatives and friends have no reason to expect any redeeming value from this infamous child. Eagerness of the child's departure is great, if not welcomed. Dishonor mounts in the hearts of those embarrassed as they ever watch the development of the youth. This behavior may or may not have continued into adulthood, so adding insult to injury. Then comes the day of enlightenment, deliverance and improvement. The child of distress and disgrace confesses his or her faults and accepts Jesus as his or her savior and begins to proclaim the gospel (good news) of Jesus to everyone, including his or her family and friends, only to be rejected.

This child, again, leaves home but this time to pursue his or her new life and the direction of God. While obeying God and the Holy Spirit's prompting, the instruction is given to return home. Their life being set apart to God has been fulfilling and exciting. Then in the heart of this child came the call from God to one of the offices of the five-fold ministry, Prophet. This once "child" of destruction, shame and insult now claims to be chosen by God to stand in an official position in the church.

Upon the entrance to their childhood dwelling, the child declares, again, the goodness of God, His majesty and love, only to repeatedly be rejected.

This level of rejection equals the reception of Jesus to His home of Nazareth. Jesus had gone forth from His childhood surroundings, but with a spotless character and spirit, to accomplish His existence and call on earth. And in His travels returned home to share the same good news that God was among them. Instead of being welcomed and honored, the neighbors were offended at His announcement. They are unable to respond in a positive manner and were non-accepting of Jesus' telling them of God's grace.

Charges and finger pointing were then cast in hostility toward Jesus from the town's people. "Isn't this the carpenter?" "Isn't he just a common ordinary fellow who makes his living with his hands like the rest of us?" "How is it that he's parading as a rabbi and miracle-worker?" Ultimately the mocking and sneering statement to top it all, "Isn't this Mary's son?"

Thus the same types of statements are cast at those, today, who profess the call of the Prophet. "Wasn't he or she the one who . . . and I went to school with such and such, how can they say they are a Prophet." Or "I saw them do . . . and they were the worst among us." As a result, confidence is given to the old saying "there is nothing new under the sun." We still kill our own.

After casting disapproval and put-downs at Jesus, the underlying truths could not be denied. None could deny the fact of His wisdom and miracles, thus condemning themselves. This brought to bear other outrage that becomes visible in such importance within their own hearts, because of their lack of faith. It is thought the people took it upon themselves to understand that they had certain special rights by being God's chosen people. That error is joined to a more serious one: resentment that Jesus had taken God's favor to others beyond Nazareth, especially Capernaum, said to have had a heavy non-Jewish population[28].

In the face of all the facts, charges, events, the breakdown of the data and unbelief we focus on why Jesus made the declaration at His generation.

Jesus went about doing good: healing the sick, raising the dead, restoring sight to the blind, while ever preaching and teaching the Words of His Father. He said I do nothing I don't see my Father do; believe on me for the works sake. Jesus was saying to all it was not for recognition that he did the miracles and spoke God's Word, but he was doing what His Father had been doing since the days of Noah, the call of Abraham and the deliverance through Moses. God desires His children to be wealthy, healthy and declaring the love, works and wonders of Himself, to the Jew first and to the Gentiles.

But Jesus was despised and rejected of men. Not only cast off and unwanted by just any people, but his blood relatives, as well as the town's people. This being so unpopular and hated, was this jealousy or envy? Was it both? Were the leaders of His day so enraged because they knew the scriptures but, for whatever reason, tradition or "created" doctrine, by the leaders of the day, had not and were not doing what was told and taught them from their birth?

Jesus was the greatest prophet of the day, even though He called John the Baptist the greatest; "there is none greater than John.[29] Jesus did many healings, miracles and taught a large quantity of the masses based on God's

---

[28] Fred B. Craddock, "Luke", Interpretation, p.63.
[29] Matthew 11:11

original intent of His Word. His illustration of the Person as the Prophet and the Office of the Prophet caused a stir and uproar among those chosen leaders, more so on tradition and family line, to lead the people.

Persons associate the Office of the Prophet and the Person as the Prophet to a level of greatness not represented by the Word of God, the office or the person. A person only will endeavor to do the will of God in the framework of his or her calling, while contained in the same boundaries as the people to whom they were sent, skin, the human body.

What is most disturbing is the rejection's prominence in one's own home, meaning one's birth or blood relatives. This rejection can be covered up within the family with the "ointment" of compassion, but surfaces with the lack of support when confronted by neighbors. The state of close relationship and intimacy, with the absence of formality, propagates the act of despising, a state of mind to despise and a lack of respect or reverence of the Prophet. We better know this concept as "familiarity breeds contempt." Man believes to be familiar is disgraceful but God, however, concepts an opposing view.

In Greek, Atimos (at'-ee-mos) is the central word representing the concept man portrays towards persons striving to obey God and those He has advanced to a separated position. The derivatives of atimos compose of 'a' meaning *without* and *Time'* meaning *honor*, therefore Atimos means dishonored, to be without honor, of low character or reputation and the definition parallels the expanded structure of the cliche'. It also carries added definitions of disdain, without recognition, despise, disrespected, without value or price, giving separation to the level of thought and stature from one's peers as below their standards. The same treatment of Jesus has gone beyond the limits of time in the similar reproach of God's separated ones today. The lack of respect held for Jesus by the town's people of Nazareth was a tangible expression of their lack of faith. This "expression of their faith" is projected towards Prophets of today.

God chooses who will share in His glory and honor, therefore let's look at glory and honor. Doxa (dox'-ah) in the Greek means *glory, splendor, radiance, fame, renown, honor, esteem, respect and reputation*. Thus God bestows upon one the level man was given before the fall. The restoration of this stature elevates the Prophet, as well as believers, to a face-to-face fellowship and relationship. Within this elevation comes the opportunity of the Prophet to participate in Jesus' glory, which is the Father's, and realize, by the power of the Holy Spirit, the same works Jesus manifested in glorifying the Father. Therefore, Prophets are the image and glory of God, through their obedience, holiness, purity, good deeds and willingness to suffer for Jesus.

Along with the glory comes the *honor*, Time' (tee-may'), therefore, raising the Prophet's value. While one's peers do not recognize this exalted status, God will confer His honor upon His vessel that is deserving for His use. So Jesus made it plain, one cannot honor the Father unless he honors the Son, and God esteems honor and respect to the Prophet despite persecution and rejection, when others will not give honor where honor is due.

CHAPTER SIX

Observations of the Learned

This chapter can be thought to be overly magnificent or grand in its presentation. The intent of these words are to allow original expression of persons that have written, either, briefly or extensively on the subject of the Prophet. In a very few cases definitions were given instead of the original written words, but in the majority of the statements the original language has been preserved, for substance, clarity and effectiveness.

In this chapter our focus will be to listen to the "pulse" of today's contemporary and past leaders. Those who are well-respected, well-known, not so well known, Christian, Islamic, theologians and the academic world.

The subject of the Prophet goes beyond cultures, seas and generations, so it would be proper for us to obtain a cross-cultural, as well as, a multi-faceted view from matured, observing eyes.

The question is and has been proposed to the learned inquiring as to the existence of prophets in present day. "For many years, the ministry of the prophet has been ignored or misunderstood. Some would even tell us that the office of the prophet has passed away. Many have thought the ministry of the prophet was limited to the Old Testament period. Or they say there were prophets in the Old Testament and in the New Testament, but there are none today." There is no scriptural evidence to demonstrate this statement since ministry gifts will be necessary until Jesus comes for His Church.

"A Prophet speaks from the impulse of a <u>sudden inspiration</u>, from the light of a sudden revelation at the moment. The idea of speaking from sudden revelation seems here to be elementary, as relating either to future events or the mind of the Spirit in general. A prophet speaks by direct divine inspiration, an immediate revelation, not something thought of, but something given at the spur of the moment by sudden inspiration."

"To stand in the office of a prophet, one is first of all a minister of the gospel, separated and called to the ministry with the calling of God upon one's life. The prophet is a ministry gift. There are no prophets among what we call laymen because a prophet is one who is called to the full-time ministry."[30]

"Also in the office of prophet, one must have a more consistent manifestation of at least two of the revelation gifts (word of wisdom, word of knowledge or discerning of spirits) plus prophecy."

"A prophet is one who speaks for God. A prophet has been given the unique ministry of representing God before men. This revelation (expression from God), while in total harmony with Scripture, will give direction, confirm guidance and vision, give insight into the Word of God, tell facts about people's lives, rebuke, judge, correct, warn and reveal future events."

"A prophet will minister under a greater level of the prophetic anointing and with greater detail and accuracy than will one who is simply operating in the spiritual gift of prophecy."

"The prophets were men who were close to God and represented God in their daily life and ministry. They were called seers because of their visions, insight and foresight of God's revelation to His people."

"The prophets as mediators were the teachers or interpreters of the law. They gave themselves more to understanding the spirit (life-source) of the law than the letter of the law. They made sense of the history of the nation in the light of the Word of the Lord."

"The ministry of the prophet involves the grounding and establishing of churches. The prophet will work together with the apostle in laying spiritual foundations for the new churches and ministries."

---

[30] Kenneth E. Hagin, The Ministry Gifts

"Prophets will be involved together with a team of ministering elders in confirming ministry giftings and in imparting and releasing the operation of the gifts of the Holy Spirit in believer's lives through the laying on of hands. They will bring the prophetic word during this special time of ministry and the prophet will always be calling the church into a closer relationship with God."[31]

"With the work the prophet does alongside and complimenting the apostle, as well the Evangelist, Pastor and Teacher, like John the Baptist prepared the way for the ministry of Jesus at His first coming to this earth, the prophets today are preparing the way for His second coming. God is revealing Himself, His plans, His purposes and His works through the ministry of the prophets. As with every major event, God will reveal the events of His Second Coming so that His Bride will be prepared and ready to unite with Jesus and leave the earth. God always reveals His plan to His people through His prophets."

To the damage of the church, many prophets have not been well received in their home church. Often churches where God has sent prophets with a true prophetic message the church bodies have not received their words. "We are warned against refusing to listen to a prophet."

"And it shall be that whoever
will not hear My words,
which He speaks in My name,
I will require it of him."[32]

His own did not receive even Jesus. And Jesus said that anyone who received a prophet as a prophet would receive a prophet's reward:

"He who receives a prophet
in the name of a prophet
shall receive a prophet's
reward, And he who
receives a righteous man
in the name of a righteous

---

[31] A. L. Gill, The Ministry Gifts
[32] Deuteronomy 18:19

27

> man shall receive a
> righteous man's reward."[33]

Many have dared to pretend to be speaking for God in order to get their own way or to control others. Others have prophesied from the wrong motivations instead of from a deep personal relationship with God.

"Some have prophesied what they have received from familiar spirits. (Due to the fact our focus in not familiar spirits, it is suggested personal investigation on the subject would better serve you versus a detour of explanation.) When this happens, speaking from the influence of familiar spirits, it's important that the gift of the distinguishing (recognizing) of spirits be in operation, then the so called revelations or prophesies can be exposed for what they are, witchcraft. God additionally warns the prophets themselves to exercise discerning of spirits and self-control."

> "And the spirits of the
> prophets are subject to the
> prophets."[34]

With this command and caution from Paul, due to the extremes displayed in the Corinthian churches, all prophets should expect, allow and give opportunity for all of their prophecies to be judged. Thus prophets are to ensure they have clear leading from the Holy Spirit to give forth a prophecy. "As humans, we are imperfect, mortal beings and subject to making mistakes, more so in <u>when</u> to present the prophecy and just because a person gives a prophecy that's not right doesn't necessarily mean that he is a false prophet."

In the early start of the nineteen hundred and nineties, it has been presented that the "priesthood is changing" and "we are shifting from the voice of the many to the Voice of the One, from the voice of the prophets to the Voice of the Son. The voices of the prophets are to be swallowed up in the Voice of the Son. The prophets were the voices of the Old Covenant; the Son is the Voice of the New Covenant. That was then; this is now."[35]

---

[33] Matthew 10:41
[34] I Corinthians 14:32
[35] Kelley Varner, The Priesthood Is Changing

This understanding gives rise to the end of the prophets. But Kelley Varner goes on to say "God is restoring the prophetic to the Church, but it must be held in the perspective of three dimensions," God, the prophets, and Jesus through the Holy Spirit, "not just two," God and the prophets. "It is passing, not permanent. Like the issue of authority and submission, the prophetic is a vehicle, a means to an end, and not the end itself. The priesthood is changing, and the streams of the prophets must flow into one river, the Voice of the Son."

He goes on to say the purpose of every godly parent, pastor or prophet is that those under their care learn to pray and listen for the Voice of the Lord.

More recently, authors and theologians have come to state; "the prophetic word and voice must be <u>recovered</u> if we are to be able to deal effectively with the original intent of the Church in our time. The WORD of the Lord creates <u>ex nihilo</u>[36] (out of nothing), and there can be no new thing unless we hear that Word."

"To truly understand the purpose and manner of the prophetic ministry and imagination, we will realize that those in prophetic ministry can discern the season in which we live and speak the "new thing" prior to its arrival. This, in essence, is <u>the purpose of the prophetic voice</u>."

"It involves the dismantling of the "old" thing that has outlived its usefulness and the calling forth of the radically "new" thing that is about to arrive."

"Prophets tell of God's intentions. The prophets see the intention of God and stands outside the standard of "the way we've always done it around here." This kind of ministry is characterized by a fresh and original revelation of the Christ and the Father's purpose in the Christ from eternity to eternity. It so grips the imagination of the prophet's soul that it causes them to call the Church to uncompromisingly extreme holiness and demand a departure from corrupt religiosity."[37]

---

[36] Mark Chironna, A Passion For the Glory
[37] condition of being religious or excessively religious

"The progressive revelation of the Christ is the core of what all true prophets can see or hear. They see the absolute Headship of the Christ and the sovereign rule of the Christ in the Body by the power of the Spirit."

Walter Breuggemann wrote:

> "The task of prophetic ministry
> is to nurture, nourish, and evoke
> a consciousness and perception
> alternative to the consciousness
> and perception of the dominant
> culture around us."

"Prophetic speech is faith-filled, history-making and prophetic words and when truly "heard" with the spirit, allow God to make us into vessels of the future fit to bear the glory of His dream which has been forgotten."

"So how does the local Pastor or Body of Elders Shepherd the Prophet? Prophetic people are not necessarily responsible for the interpretation of their words and definitely not responsible for the application of them. That responsibility lies with the leaders or with the individual or group to whom the prophecy is given." "Prophecy, as aforementioned, is a sudden, divine impulse statement. The content is given with the express purpose of confirming a directive or instruction. The corporate body, individuals or individual should give confidence and acceptance to the prophecy should they choose to reveal if the prophecy is accurate. No prophet should question or inquire to the soundness of the prophecy, again the "witness" or knowledge and understanding of the prophecy would be spiritual. This would then constitute the receiver(s) to seek God to obtain acceptance and confidence and/or assistance for the interpretation or compliance."

"With this in mind, prophets, like any child of God, should have a "church home" and all prophetic people must cultivate a heart of submission. Having a church home, being submitted to a local authority, will aide in the avoidance of pride."

"Prophetic people need to know they are only responsible before God to express what they believe the Lord is saying. They are not responsible to see that directional words are carried out." Prophetic people may be rejected. As we saw in chapter five, the issue of familiarity can raise its ugly head.

Let's step across the cultural and theological lines. In the strict Jewish understanding of the concept of a prophet, Abraham J. Heschel defines the prophet more obscure and, in some ways, bizarre.

"Prophets will throw followers into orations about widows and orphans, about the corruption of judges and affairs of the market place. Instead of showing us a way through the elegant mansions of the mind, the prophets take us to the slums. The world is a proud place, full of beauty, but the prophets are scandalized, and rave as if the whole world were a slum. They make much ado about paltry[38] things, lavishing excessive language upon trifling subjects."

"To a person endowed with prophetic sight, everyone else appears blind; to a person whose ear perceives God's voice, everyone else appears deaf. No one is just; no knowing is strong enough, no trust complete enough. The prophet hates the approximate; he shuns the middle of the road. Man must live on the peak (high point) to avoid the emptiness. There is nothing to hold to except God. Carried away by the challenge, the demand to straighten out man's ways, the prophet is strange, one-sided, an unbearable extremist."

"Others may suffer from the terror of cosmic aloneness; the prophet is overwhelmed by the grandeur of divine presence. He is incapable of isolating the world. There is an interaction between man and God which to disregard is an act of disrespect."

"The prophet disdains those for whom God's presence is comfort and security; to him it is a challenge, an never-ending demand."

"The prophet is a watchman, a servant, a messenger of God, "an assayer and tester" of the people's ways.[39] The prophet's eye is directed to the contemporary scene; the society and its conduct are the main theme of his speeches. Yet his ear is inclined to God. He is a person struck by the glory and presence of God, overpowered by the hand of God." To contrast this definition in an interview with Seyyed Hossein Nasr, a Professor of Islamic studies, Seyyed says "a prophet is someone who is the harbinger[40] of news from the Divine, who brings something to us from the Divine." This statement brings the concept and position of the prophet back to the Old

---

[38] Definition: Inferior; trashy; mean; despicable; trivial; meager; measly
[39] Jeremiah 6:27
[40] One that warns of the future; foreshadows what is to come

Testament definition and description as in chapter two. "So the idea of the connectedness of the prophet to God and the bringing of news, which is knowledge of something which concerns us, is contained in the etymology of the word prophet in Arabic."

"A prophet is chosen by God from on high; you cannot develop yourself into becoming a prophet. In contrast to being a great mystic, metaphysician or philosopher, you can neither undergo formal external training, nor even inner purification to become a prophet. God chooses a prophet."

With all that said, it brings things down to the controversy that stirs the pot of disharmony in the church.

"Some do not believe that personal prophecy is scriptural. They do not believe that a prophet may have a message for an individual. Even though Agabus had a personal prophecy for Paul. He did not tell Paul not to go to Jerusalem, he merely told Paul what would happen should Paul go to Jerusalem.

"Under the New Covenant it is not a scriptural base to seek guidance through the ministry of the prophet and many think that a prophet is supposed to do nothing but prophecy, but the foremost ministry of the prophet is to preach or teach the Word." "The Lord only tells a prophet what He wants them to know. God does not tell a prophet everything. The prophet will give warnings, which can provide protection for God's people. These warnings can prepare them for what lies ahead, just as He, the Holy Spirit, does with the inner witness."

"So the ministry of the prophet brings strengthening, encouragement and comfort. But it is felt that this does not define out to other than a "feel good" prophecy." On the contrary, as elaborated upon in chapter three, prophecy encompasses much more. "Thus even as the prophets Haggai and Zechariah encouraged the people to rebuild the ruins, the prophet today will be continually encouraging, motivating and exciting the people to finish the work of God, while Nathans will come along to re-direct the ones who may stray or just blatantly disobey."

An expose' in Christianity Today contained a depiction of what discord on prophecy can result. Some persons were hurt, unfortunately, but as it can be said, "don't throw the baby out with the bath water."

Pastor Mike Bickle, and prophets such as Bob Jones, John Paul Jackson, and Paul Cain and their church, Kansas City Fellowship (KCF) claims that the prophetic gift should be restored in the church. They state prophecy is a natural, biblical means for God to speak to his people, and that (here's the apocalyptic part) this increased prophetic activity is a sign of the emergence of the last-days' victorious church.

Wayne Grudem, author of <u>The Gift of Prophecy in the New Testament and Today</u>, who teaches theology at Trinity Evangelical Divinity School and attends a small Vineyard-affiliated church, argues that every prophet today will make mistakes. The corresponding role of Old Testament prophets, who could not make mistakes without being declared false and put to death,[41] in the New Testament are not prophets but apostles. Paul's injunction to test all prophecy assumes there will be some error.[42] He even says that prophecies are now imperfect.[43] According to the New Testament diagram for the church, prophets are to be subject to teacher/elders who are entrusted with the leadership of the church.[44] The purpose of prophecy in the New Testament is to upbuild, encourage and console[45], and not to speak "the very words of God," even if the words are 100-percent accurate. Grudem—and KCF and Vineyard leaders agree—there is a discontinuity between the canonical revelation found in the Bible and the revelation received by modern-day prophets.

A critic of Grudem, Robert Thomas, who teaches New Testament at California's Master's Seminary, believes Grudem has "made far too big a discontinuity between New and Old Testament prophecy" and Grudem has not overcome one basic theological obstacle, "How can you have inspired utterance that has error?" "That is a contradiction in terms."

Michael G. Maudlin concluded the article by saying, "I am reminded of Gamaliel's words:

---

[41] Deuteronomy 18:20-22
[42] I Thessalonians 5:20-21
[43] I Corinthians 13:10
[44] I Peter 5:5; Acts 20:17
[45] I Corinthians 14:3

"If their purpose or activity
is of human origin, it will fail.
But if it is from God, you will
not be able to stop these men"[46].

It can be said that the Church is going the way of the Pharisees with the strict adherence to the law. Paul told us, however, that the letter kills but the Spirit makes alive. Those who live by the letter have a need for everything to be known and manageable, but the life of God moves beyond the borders of human management. Prophetic ministry does not deal with the "letter" as it is known. It recognizes that the life of the Spirit carries the element of surprise and amazement.

"The prophetically motivated individual or community will often raise more questions than they answer, because they are immersed in the power of God's creative expression. It is not that the prophet challenges the law, but rather the revealing belief of those who have used the law to manipulate and coerce others to do things their way."

True prophetic ministry always seems to call into question the status quo. It is sometimes so radical in nature that the status quo will call the prophetic anything but God; Jesus was called a "blasphemer" and "Beelzebub," while Paul was given the privilege of being called a "heretic."

"The Church has yet to fully comprehend the foundational truth of the prophetic ministry, understand the prophetic gift is essential to the work of God in the Church and for that reason there is a desperate need for the restoration of prophetic preaching in the land. It is the "foolishness of preaching" that must regain a primacy in the world. Preaching by men and women with prophetic conviction, who are not ashamed of the cross, indeed is the power of God that will issue forth in salvation."

There is yet the full thought and intention of God to be realized in the earth and there is a need to call the people of God to rise out of mediocrity into the greatness of God's glory with a passion for His presence. For those with a sense of the glorious future in store for the Church of the living God, those who are prophetically tempered, motivated, gifted or called, the only consolation is the promise of God's abiding presence.

---

[46] Acts 5:38-39

CHAPTER SEVEN

Final Thoughts and Opinions

During the travels of these pages you may have heard the "pain" of one that is called to stand in the office, which has been presented. You may hear the anguish of love desired; that the body of Christ recalls the goodness and mercy that can be afforded through the Prophet's ministry. The cries of one Prophet or many entreating for the lives passing through the atmosphere of challenge and for the world that was deceitfully acquired from the creation of love, mankind, fashioned by the God of the universe.

The Prophet, like John the Baptist, is one crying in the wilderness against the disobedience to the Word of God and the lack of understanding confined in the minds of the "enlightened" of the things of God.

At the opening of this view we looked at what God dropped into the head of the writer to persuade thought upon the scriptures that have not ended. God, through His servant the Prophet, desires that our "eyes be enlightened"[47] to the depths of His heart. God's word still states, "till heaven and earth pass, one jot or one tittle shall in no wise pass from the law[48], till all be fulfilled."[49]

Contained in this approach is my intent to present why I believe that some in the church body and or people reject Prophets and the existence of the Office in the modern church as a likely office and as an official officer and elder. Afterward the targets explored are some mistaken beliefs about

---

[47] Ephesians 1:18
[48] Canon, doctrine, ordinance, precept, principle, rule
[49] Matthew 5:18

the Office of the Prophet and the Person as the Prophet, while rounding out the proposal with prophecy and the charges cast by Jesus in the gospels[50].

Through exploration of the Old Testament and New Testament Prophet, there were the discovered changes in operations God made of the functions each communicate. God in His infinite wisdom made the noteworthy announcement that He would raise up a Prophet from among the nation, Israel, He has singled out from among the nations and called. God raises up, today; from within His children Prophets to lead and guide them back to the throne of grace (unmerited, unearned favor) and God's face. These people are called to stand in an office of and in strong conviction. Due to the importance of the position, continually they are declaring and exposing sin (transgression of the commandments of God, error and disobedience) to the world and believers, that God is not pleased with their ways but still loves them and is calling His creation to righteousness.

While showing the New Testament Prophet does not receive any new revelation opposite of the Word, hopefully it has been shown they do receive divine revelation just as the Old Testament Prophet and are divinely inspired. Thus the question of whether they are God inspired can be said to be given soundness, as well as the uncertainty as to whether were they chosen. Thus, based on the facts and information presented, the New Testament Prophet is set apart for and to the work of ministry, also in a decision-making and managerial position, and are called of God.

The question of prophecy or stumbling block in the acceptance and carrying out of prophecy is satisfied, in my opinion, based solely on the scriptures. The Book of First Corinthians clearly states the gifts of the Holy Spirit are present and functioning in the church body today. Since the scriptures will never pass away until fulfilled, prophecies will continue to be spoken forth and completed. Granted there has been error in a variety of areas, timing of a prophecy, to whom the prophecy is directed and whether a prophecy is individual or community wide, but there does not appear to be enough widespread evidence to disagree with prophecy's existence.

Additional error has been brought about by those entering the work of ministry for questionable motives or as scripture states, filthy lucre, better

---

[50] Matthew 13:57; Mark 6:4 and John 4:44

known as greed. There have been those, whether genuine or non-genuine, using the gift of prophecy to control and pressure people with the sole focus of financial gain. Scripture has plainly warned against the "love of money"[51] as a focus of entering ministry. One's central desire, in life as a whole, should be to glorify, praise and exalt the name of Jesus. But like salvation, everyone is called with a need to stand before God for themselves to account for what was said, not said, done or not done in their calling, because only that which is done for the sake of the calling of Jesus will stand.

In chapter four and five the "hurt" felt by some whom accepted the call from Father God is more readily brought to the surface. By separating the Office of the Prophet from the Person of the Prophet, I was hoping something would materialize as to the reasons for negative responses, mainly where people clash most, in their personalities. Some people are incapable of distinguishing the person from the person's function and in so doing throw out "the baby with the bath water." When a person is given the ability to look at each component of something they may be more willing to accept the item. This breaking down of the Office of the Prophet from the Person of the Prophet may cause more examination by persons performing the research to assist them in the removal of self-formulated and man-made prejudice.

In Unwelcome (chapter five), again, the exposure of prejudice is the focus and this time on a more intimate level. The adaptation was a short scenario to show that people who have not been trained by "life", family, religious influence or are just not what society would choose, God will take the

> . . . "foolish things of the world to confound the wise; and God hath chosen the weak things of the world to confound the things which are mighty."[52]

---

[51] 1 Timothy 6:10
[52] 1 Corinthians 1:27

God looks at the area of man no one but the Holy Spirit and the spirit of a man can know: one's spirit. Then God will go even farther to show His favor upon His obedient, yielded servant by sharing His glory and honor with them.[53] God is declaring to all that observe their life, through His glory and honor, He is pleased with His vessel that lays down their life and agenda, serves and is obedient.

In chapter six we listened to scholar's and teacher's thoughts and opinions, a majority of which I am in agreement. I take exception with the thought of the Prophet having ceased due to the thought of "the priesthood is changing."[54] Then the Physician Luke was mentioned in chapter two to have made reference in Acts of the coming out of Prophets. Since Jesus has stated,

> "It was he who gave some to be
> apostles, some to be prophets,
> some to be evangelists, and
> some to be pastors and teachers,
> to prepare God's people for works
> of service, so that the body of
> Christ may be built up until we all
> reach unity in the faith and in the
> knowledge of the Son of God and
> become mature, attaining to the
> whole measure of the fullness
> of Christ"[55],

how then can our standing as Priests (Prophets) cease to exist? I am unclear on the opinion of the "many voices to the Voice of One" since, in my understanding, the many have only been one, just multiple persons, but the Voice of One. Then the distinction of "the Prophets to the Voice of One" appears to relate the same thought just re-worded. I must, by necessity, say again God's Word will not pass away until all (that which God has declared

---

[53] 1 Samuel 2:30 and John 12:26

[54] Varner, Kelley, The Preisthood Is Changing. Pennsylvania: Destiny Image Publishers. 1991.

[55] Ephesians 4:11-13, New International Version

to come to final result) has been completed and His children are praising His name in <u>One</u> Voice.

The "contrasting religions" seem to correspond with the Christian communities' understanding of the Prophet, just more cautious or uncertain in the Prophet's foundation and source. Still other religions being more "mystical" in their approach may prompt caution, but the heart of the calling, i.e. divine, remains identical.

What happens if we continue in the frame of thought that causes a person to be of two minds on the truth of the Word? The understanding should well be to not accept all of the written Word of God is to not accept all of God. Since Genesis chapter one no purpose of God has diminished, we just haven't completed and obeyed. Jesus stated He came to complete the law not destroy the law. But we have been given a more excellent word and that word still contains obedience to the <u>whole</u> Word. Are there any outcomes to not accepting and doing the whole Word?

Therefore, in this writer's opinion, and based on the knowledge I received from my studies, the majority being received from God's Word, the Person as the Prophet and the Office of the Prophet are active and practical units of the church body, Jesus' Bride.

I believe it would enhance the Body of Jesus and it would do all well to go back to the Scriptures, combined with their knees, to seek the whole truth for themselves. Those that endeavor to take hold of this challenge are thus creating evidence and support of being a living epistle capable of stating, "I studied to show myself approved."[56] This will in turn bestow upon us the ability to hear on that great day from our Father God of whom we desire to please and praise, "well done thou good and faithful servant."

---

[56] II Timothy 2:15

To schedule speaking engagements, Bible Studies, Elisha conferences and information on the annual "I AM" conference contact:

Angelic Messenger Ministries
5025 North Central Avenue
Suite 348
Phoenix, Arizona 85012
(602) 810-7101

or

Email: the1stmessenger@msn.com
Webpage: angelicmessenger.org

BIBLIOGRAPHY

Anonymous, <u>Exegetical Dictionary of the New Testament</u>, Edited by Horst Balz and Gerhard Schneider. Michigan: William B. Eerdmans Publishing Company. 1993.

Boice, James Montgomery and A. Sjevingon Wood, "Galatians and Ephesians", <u>The Expositor's Bible Commentary</u>, Edited by Frank E. Gaebelein, J. D. Douglas and Richard P. Polcyn. Michigan: Zondervan Publishing House. 1995.

Campbell, Wesley, "Pastoring the Prophetic", <u>Ministries Today</u>, XIV, (September/October 1996), 45-49.

Carson, D. A., "Matthew, Chapters 13 through 28", <u>The Expositor's Bible Commentary</u>, Edited by Frank E. Gaebelein, J. D. Douglas and Richard P. Polcyn. Michigan: Zondervan Publishing House. 1995.

Chironna, Mark, <u>A Passion For the Glory</u>. Okalahoma: Vincom Publishing Company. 1996.

Craddock, Fred B., "Luke", <u>Interpretation, A Bible Commentary For Teaching and Preaching</u>. Kentucky: John Knox Press. 1990.

Fausset, Andrew Robert, <u>Bible Cyclopaedia</u>, Critical and Expository. Connecticut: The S. S. Scranton Company. 1907.

Gilbrant, Thoralf, and Tor Inge Gilbrant, "The Greek-English Dictionary", <u>The Complete Biblical Library</u>, 1991, Volume 15. Missouri: The Complete Biblical Library. 1992.

_____, "Study Bible, Matthew", <u>The Complete Biblical Library</u>, 1986, Volume 2. Missouri: The Complete Biblical Library. 1989.

_____, "Study Bible, Mark", <u>The Complete Biblical Library</u>, 1986, Volume 3. Missouri: The Complete Biblical Library. 1988.

_____, "Study Bible, Luke", <u>The Complete Biblical Library</u>, 1986, Volume 4. Missouri: The Complete Biblical Library. 1988.

Gill, A. L., The Ministry Gifts Apostles, Prophets, Evangelists, Pastors, Teachers. California: Powerhouse Publishing. 1989,1995.

Hailey, Homer, A Commentary on The Minor Prophets. Religious Supply, Inc. 1993.

Harris, R. Laird, Gleason L. Archer, Jr. and Bruce K. Waltke, Theological Wordbook of the Old Testament, Volume 2. Chicago: The Moody Bible Institute. 1980.

Heschel, Abraham J., "What Manner of Man is the Prophet", Parabola, XXI, (Spring 1996), 6-9.

Liefield, Walter L., "Luke", The Expositor's Bible Commentary, Edited by Frank E. Gaebelein, J. D. Douglas and Richard P. Polcyn. Michigan: Zondervan Publishing House. 1995.

Maudlin, Michael G., "Seers in the Heartland", Christianity Today, XXXV, (January 1991), 18-22.

Mounce, Robert H., "Matthew", New International Biblical Commentary, Volume 1. Massachusetts: Hendrickson Publishers, Inc. 1991.

Nasr, Seyyed Hossein, "The First Prophet", Parabola, XXI, (Spring 1996), 13-19.

Robertson, Archibald Thomas, Word Pictures in the New Testament, Volume 1. Michigan: Baker Book House. 1930.

Scheidler, Bill, The New Testament Church and Its Ministries. Oregon: Bible Temple Publishing. 1980.

Varner, Kelley, The Priesthood Is Changing. Pennsylvania: Destiny Image Publishers. 1991.

Vine, W. E., The Expanded Vine's Expository Dictionary of New Testament Words, edited by John R. Kohlenberger III with James A. Swanson. Minnesota: Bethany House Publishers. 1984.

Wessel, Walter W., "Mark", The Expositor's Bible Commentary, Edited by Frank E. Gaebelein, J. D. Douglas and Richard P. Polcyn. Michigan: Zondervan Publishing House. 1995.

Williams, J. Rodman, "Salvation, the Holy Spirit, and Christian Living", Renewal Theology. Volume 2. Michigan: Zondervan Publishing House. 1990.

————————, "The Church, the Kingdom, and the Last Things", <u>Renewal Theology</u>. Volume 3. Michigan: Zondervan Publishing House. 1992.

Wuest, Kenneth S., <u>Word Studies in the Greek New Testament</u>, Volume 1. Michigan: William B. Eerdmans Publishing Company. 1973. Reprinted 1994.

Printed in the United States
By Bookmasters